LIGHTNING BOLT BOOKS™

Taking Care of Your Horse

Lisa Idzikowski

Lerner Publications ◆ Minneapolis

For My Family

Lerner Publications Company
An imprint of Lerner Publishing Group, Inc.
241 First Avenue North
Minneapolis, MN 55401 USA

For reading levels and more information, look up this title at www.lernerbooks.com.

Main body text set in Billy Infant Regular. Typeface provided by SparkType.

Library of Congress Cataloging-in-Publication Data

Names: Idzikowski, Lisa, author.
Title: Taking care of your horse / Lisa Idzikowski.
Description: Minneapolis, Minneapolis : Lerner Publications, [2025] | Series: Lightning bolt books—Horse lover's library | Includes bibliographical references and index. | Audience: Ages 6-9 | Audience: Grades 2-3 | Summary: "From grooming to getting exercise, horses need a lot of care. Young readers also learn how to stay safe around horses. Discover more about what horses need to be happy and healthy"— Provided by publisher.
Identifiers: LCCN 2023036898 (print) | LCCN 2023036899 (ebook) | ISBN 9798765626085 (library binding) | ISBN 9798765628928 (paperback) | ISBN 9798765635001 (epub)
Subjects: LCSH: Horses—Juvenile literature. | Horses—Health—Juvenile literature.
Classification: LCC SF302 .I398 2025 (print) | LCC SF302 (ebook) | DDC 636.1—dc23/eng/20230824

LC record available at https://lccn.loc.gov/2023036898
LC ebook record available at https://lccn.loc.gov/2023036899

Manufactured in the United States of America
1-1009873-51942-10/13/2023

Table of Contents

Lots of Care

A boy feeds his horse. The horse munches on its food. Many people with horses love to see them happy with a full belly.

Horses need food, fresh water, and exercise. They also need a safe place to live and room to roam.

Having a horse is a lot of work. Their stalls need to be cleaned every day.

Safety

Part of caring for horses is staying safe. Always go with a trusted adult to see a horse.

Horses scare easily. To keep them calm, move slowly and don't make loud noises.

You can gently pet a horse's snout.

Approach horses from their side. Talk quietly as you get close.

Never go behind a horse. It could kick. Always wear shoes that cover your toes.

Horses respond well to steady, gentle voices and movements.

Feeding Your Horse

Horses graze much of the day. A horse in a pasture can munch on plants. Horses inside stalls eat hay.

Horses need more to eat when they work hard or exercise. They might be fed grain such as oats twice a day in addition to hay and grazing.

An average-sized horse eats about 20 pounds (9 kg) of food each day.

All horses need clean water. Most horses drink between 5 to 10 gallons (19 to 38 L) of water each day.

Horses need more water if it's hot outside or if they have been exercising.

Many horses have pastures and stables. They eat inside their stalls.

Healthy at Home

Horses should be able to get in the barn from the pasture. Then they can be protected from the weather and predators.

Some brushes are only for certain parts of the horse's body.

Many people groom their horses at least once a week. You should clean their hooves and brush their hair.

Horses feel best when they exercise. Horses with pastures might get enough exercise from walking around. Horses mainly kept in stalls need to be taken out for exercise.

Riding a horse is one way to exercise them.

Veterinarians and farriers care for horses. Horses see vets for yearly checkups and when sick or hurt.

Horses see farriers to get new horseshoes or trimmed hooves.

Taking good care of a horse keeps it happy and healthy.

Taking Care of Your Horse and You

Horses can need a lot of care. If you had a horse, what would be your favorite part of caring for your animal?

Fun Facts

- Horses are herbivores and eat only plants.
- Horses have two sets of teeth in their life, baby teeth and adult teeth.
- A horse's hooves grow constantly, just like fingernails.

Glossary

farrier: a person who trims horses' hooves and places shoes on their hooves

graze: to eat grass or other plants that are growing in a field

hay: grass that has been cut and dried to be used as food for animals

pasture: a large area of land where animals feed on grass

predator: an animal that lives by killing and eating other animals

stall: an enclosed area in a building where a farm animal is kept

veterinarian: a person who is trained to give medical care and treatment to animals

weather: temperature and other outside conditions at a certain time and place

Learn More

Britannica Kids: Horse
https://kids.britannica.com/kids/article/horse/353265

Krenn, Cara. *Horseback Riding*. Minneapolis: Lerner Publications, 2025.

Pang, Ursula. *Horse Farms*. New York: PowerKids, 2023.

Pearson, Marie. *Horse Behavior*. Minneapolis: Abdo, 2023.

Rutgers: Equine Science 4 Kids!
https://esc.rutgers.edu/es4kids/

SPCA Kids: Horses
https://kids.spcaeducation.org.nz/animal-care/horses/

Index

Photo Acknowledgments

Image credits: FluxFactory/Getty Images, pp. 4, 20; PeopleImages/Getty Images, p. 5; nullplus/Getty Images, p. 6; Jupiterimages/Getty Images, p. 7; Paul Bradbury/Getty Images, p. 8; Westend61/Getty Images, p. 9; Svetlana Repnitskaya/Getty Images, p. 10; beklaus/Getty Images, p. 11; moodboard/Getty Images, p. 12; Kit Houghton/Getty Images, p. 13; alexeys/Getty Images, p. 14; Elenathewise/Getty Images, p. 15; Maskot/Getty Images, pp. 16, 20; Lane Oatey/Blue Jean Images/Getty Images, p. 17; Betsie Van Der Meer/Getty Images, p. 18; Caia Image/Getty Images, p. 19.

Cover: Tim Platt/Getty Images.